D1240079

transforming
questions
PARTICIPANT'S GUIDE

ISBN 978-0-88028-419-6

© Forward Movement, 2015

412 Sycamore Street, Cincinnati, OH 45202-4195

The *Participant's Guide* is a companion to the
Transforming Questions course, which has been
supported by a generous grant from The Episcopal
Church's Constable Fund. *Transforming Questions*
was written by Melody Wilson Shobe and Scott Gunn.

Scripture citations refer to the New Revised Standard
Version Bible, although any version is appropriate.

www.forwardmovement.org

Welcome to *Transforming Questions!* Whether you are new to the Christian faith or a longtime church member seeking a refresher, this is the place for you. Over the next few weeks, you will be invited to engage in faithful questioning with the companionship of a leader and in the midst of a community.

In this course, as you gather for table fellowship, teaching, and conversation, you will wrestle with some of the most basic questions of our faith: Who is Jesus? Does God answer prayer? Why do bad things happen? In the act of asking these questions, we hope you will see your faith transform, deepening and developing from something simple and superficial to something complicated and rich. And perhaps, in the act of asking questions, you might see yourself transformed, as the answers that you find, or the new questions that you discover, demand that you respond, changing not only what you think but also how you live. It's an exciting journey: full of twists and turns, ups and downs, as you wrestle anew with your faith.

This book is your companion to the *Transforming Questions* course, a kind of guidebook for the journey. In the pages that follow, you'll find an outline of each class session, which includes references to the Bible passages and quotations that you will hear each week. We hope this will allow you to listen, follow along, and perhaps return to read and reflect on what you've heard. We've also included space for you to take notes, jot down additional questions, or add your own reflections. At the end of each outline are the discussion questions that you will explore in your small groups.

So come, you who are seekers and you who are members, you who are old and you who are young, you who are questioning for the first time and you who are questioning for the thousandth time. Together may you find that you share the same questions; together may you discover, not easy answers, but the still, small voice of God speaking in your very midst.

Melody Wilson Shobe & Scott Gunn

SESSION

1

CAN WE QUESTION OUR FAITH?

OPENING PRAYER

O God, by whom the meek are guided in judgment, and light rises up in darkness for the godly: Grant us, in all our doubts and uncertainties, the grace to ask what you would have us to do, that the Spirit of wisdom may save us from all false choices, and that in your light we may see light, and in your straight path may not stumble; through Jesus Christ our Lord. **Amen.**

(*The Book of Common Prayer,* p. 832)

Confronting misconceptions

❖ Faith as opposite of doubt

❖ Faith as blind acceptance, without questioning

Biblical witness of questioning and doubt

❖ Abraham and Sarah (Genesis 15:1-15)

❖ Moses (Exodus 3:4-15; 4:1-17)

❖ David/psalmist

   – Psalm 13:1-2

   – Psalm 22:1-2

   – Psalm 44:23-24

   – Psalm 121:1

   – Psalm 139:7

❖ Mary (Luke 1:26-38)

❖ Thomas (John 20:24-29)

❖ Paul (Acts 22:6-11)

❖ Even Jesus himself! (Matthew 27:45-50)

NOTES _____

_____

_____

_____

_____

Questions as expression of faithfulness

- ❖ Questions as part of relationship
- ❖ Questions as a way to grow
- ❖ Questions as part of being a student ("disciple")
- ❖ Questions as a form of learning (Catechism)

The opposite extreme of "never question" is "question everything"

- ❖ Taking questioning too far
- ❖ Questions as weapons
- ❖ Questions as tests
- ❖ Questions for their own sake

Faithful questioning by Jacob

- ❖ Genesis 32:22-31
- ❖ Proximity
- ❖ Hands-on
- ❖ Long term
- ❖ Possibly unanswered

NOTES _____

_____

_____

So, how can we question faithfully?

❖ We ask questions in community.
❖ We ask questions of God.
❖ We ask questions, consulting a variety of sources.

Small groups

❖ Read the story of Nicodemus (John 3:1-12; 19:38-42)
  as a group. Explore the following questions:
    – What kinds of questions is this person asking?
    – Does he receive answers to his question?
    – How does asking questions impact his faith and actions?
    – What in this person's story do you identify with?
    – How does this person's story challenge you?
❖ What questions do you bring to this class?
❖ Have you ever been reluctant to ask your questions of faith?
  Why or why not?
❖ What are you hoping to get from the next nine sessions?

NOTES _____

_____

_____

_____

How can we question faithfully?

SESSION

2

Who is Jesus?

OPENING PRAYER

Almighty God, whom truly to know is everlasting life: Grant us so perfectly to know your Son Jesus Christ to be the way, the truth, and the life, that we may steadfastly follow his steps in the way that leads to eternal life; through Jesus Christ your Son our Lord, who lives and reigns with you, in the unity of the Holy Spirit, one God, for ever and ever. **Amen.**

(*The Book of Common Prayer*, p. 225)

Historically, who is Jesus?

❖ Tacitus and Suetonius
❖ Josephus
❖ Agreement among many groups that Jesus was
  a historical person
  – That he lived
  – That he was a "good person"
  – That he was a "prophet"
  – That he died

Unique claim of Christianity

❖ That Jesus was a historical person—and also God
❖ That he lived, died, and was resurrected

Sources for Christian belief

❖ What Jesus said about himself
  – John 5:17-18; 8:58; 10:30
  – Mark 2:5-7 and Isaiah 43:25
  – Mark 14:61-62
  – "I am" statements
  – His claims about himself were so audacious,
    that they led to his death (John 10:33)

❖ What others said and believed about Jesus
  – Peter (Matthew 16:16), Thomas (John 20:28),
    the centurion (Mark 15:39)
  – Paul (Acts 9:1-20)
  – Saints through time

C.S. Lewis

❖ "I am trying here to prevent anyone saying the really foolish thing that people often say about Him: I'm ready to accept Jesus as a great moral teacher, but I don't accept his claim to be God. That is the one thing we must not say. A man who was merely a man and said the sort of things Jesus said would not be a great moral teacher. He would either be a lunatic—on the level with the man who says he is a poached egg—or else he would be the Devil of Hell. You must make your choice. Either this man was, and is, the Son of God, or else a madman or something worse. You can shut him up for a fool, you can spit at him and kill him as a demon or you can fall at his feet and call him Lord and God, but let us not come with any patronizing nonsense about his being a great human teacher. He has not left that open to us. He did not intend to." *(Mere Christianity)*

❖ Others have summarized this theological quandary, this "trilemma," by simplifying
  – Jesus is either lunatic, liar, or Lord.
  – He's either mad, bad, or good.

In the end, the question is not "Who is Jesus?" but "Who do you say that I am?"

❖ Matthew 16:13-17

Small groups

❖ What do you think is the most persuasive argument for Jesus?

❖ What is your biggest doubt or question about the reality of Jesus being the Son of God?

❖ Does C.S. Lewis' trilemma help you wrestle with the question of who Jesus is? How so or why not?

❖ Before today, how would you have answered the question, "Who is Jesus?"

❖ How do you answer the question, "Who do you say that I am?"

NOTES _____

_____

_____

_____

_____

_____

_____

_____

_____

_____

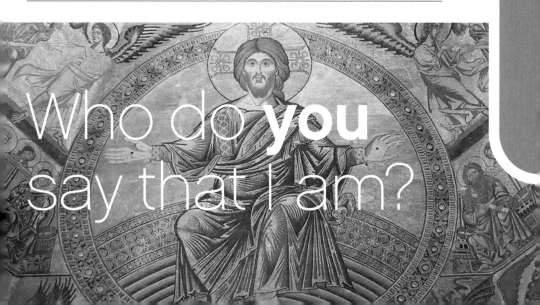

Who do **you** say that I am?

SESSION 3

Why did Jesus have to die?

OPENING PRAYER

Lord Jesus Christ, Son of the living God, we pray you to set your passion, cross, and death between your judgment and our souls, now and in the hour of our death. Give mercy and grace to the living; pardon and rest to the dead; to your holy Church peace and concord; and to us sinners everlasting life and glory; for with the Father and the Holy Spirit you live and reign, one God, now and for ever. **Amen.**

(*The Book of Common Prayer,* p. 282)

Why did Jesus have to die?

- ❖ A difficult question asked by people of all ages from the beginning of Christian history
- ❖ Area of theology called "atonement"

Centrality of Jesus' death for belief

- ❖ Cross as the symbol of our faith
- ❖ Story of death and crucifixion central to the gospels
- ❖ Jesus predicted his death many times
- ❖ The rest of the New Testament spends a lot of time talking about Jesus' death

Biblical metaphors for Jesus' death

- ❖ Redeem or ransom us from slavery
  - Galatians 4:4-7
  - Matthew 20:28
- ❖ Satisfy or pay our debt
  - Romans 6:23
- ❖ Atone for our guilt (substitutionary penal atonement)
  - Isaiah 53:5
  - 1 Peter 2:24
- ❖ Cleanse our sin
  - Hebrews 9:14

❖ Metaphors express the idea that Jesus saves us
- – From evil
- – From death
- – From ourselves

Death as a choice

❖ Scripture says that Jesus chose to die
- – John 10:17-18
- – Matthew 26:52-56
❖ Why does Jesus choose to die?
- – John 15:12-13
- – 1 John 4:9-10
- – Romans 8:31-39
- – Ephesians 1:17-21
- – Saint John Chrysostom's Easter sermon

Changing the conversation

❖ From us to God
❖ From sin to love
❖ From reasons to results

Small groups

❖ Before today, how would you have answered the question, "Why did Jesus have to die?"

❖ Does it change the way you think about Jesus' death if you ask "Why did Jesus choose to die?" instead of "Why did Jesus have to die?" If so, how so?

❖ Which of the metaphors about Jesus' death is most helpful to you? Why?

❖ Which of the metaphors about Jesus' death is most difficult for you? Why?

❖ Knowing that Jesus chose to die, for love of you, how are you feeling called to live, for love of him?

NOTES _____

_____

_____

_____

_____

_____

_____

_____

_____

Why did Jesus choose to die?

SESSION

4

What do we have to do?

OPENING PRAYER

Almighty God our heavenly Father, you declare your glory and show forth your handiwork in the heavens and in the earth: Deliver us in our various occupations from the service of self alone, that we may do the work you give us to do in truth and beauty and for the common good; for the sake of him who came among us as one who serves, your Son Jesus Christ our Lord, who lives and reigns with you and the Holy Spirit, one God, for ever and ever. **Amen.**

(*The Book of Common Prayer,* p. 261)

The realization that Jesus chose to die for love of us begs the question: How are we called to live for love of him? What do I have to do to be a Christian?

There are lots of answers to these questions:

❖ Ten Commandments (Exodus 20:1-17, Deuteronomy 5:6-21)
❖ Jesus' "add on" to the Ten Commandments (Matthew 19:16-21)
❖ The Greatest Commandment (Matthew 22:34-40 via Deuteronomy 6:5, Leviticus 19:18)
❖ The New Commandment (John 13:34-35)

That's all well and good but...

❖ That seems like a pretty high calling!
❖ And how does that love get lived out in practice?
   – When I'm stuck in traffic or buying groceries
   – When I'm in the voting booth or at the soccer field
   – When I'm attending church and when I'm not
   – When I'm with family or friends or strangers

Christians throughout the centuries have wrestled with this question. In The Episcopal Church, our liturgy proclaims what lives of love look like in the *Baptismal Covenant.*

❖ Will you continue in the apostles' teaching and fellowship, in the breaking of bread, and in the prayers?

❖ Will you persevere in resisting evil, and, whenever you fall into sin, repent and return to the Lord?

❖ Will you proclaim by word and example the Good News of God in Christ?

❖ Will you seek and serve Christ in all persons, loving your neighbor as yourself?

❖ Will you strive for justice and peace among all people, and respect the dignity of every human being? (*The Book of Common Prayer,* pp. 304-305)

That's pretty daunting; in fact it's impossible.

❖ If living this kind of life is dependent on us, then we will fail.

❖ But the response of the Baptismal Covenant is just as important as the questions asked: "I will, with God's help."

As Christians, we do not engage in the practices of our faith alone, but we are fueled by and filled with the very power of God, the Holy Spirit living and working in us.

❖ When he dies, Jesus promises that he will not leave his followers, will not leave us, alone. (John 14:15-20)

❖ The Holy Spirit fills the community of believers and empowers them to do all sorts of wonderful things. (Acts 2:1-47)

❖ That same Spirit is what abides in us and allows us to fulfill the promises of our baptism. (Ephesians 3:14-20)

Knowing that the presence and power of the Holy Spirit are with us, assured that all the promises of baptism are not something that we must do with our own strength but something that we get to do "with God's help," our question and perspective change.

❖ "What do we have to do for God?" becomes "What can we do with God in us?"

❖ "How should I now live?" is instead "How can I now live?"

❖ "What do I have to do?" becomes "What can I do, with God's help?"

Small groups

❖ When you hear the question, "What do Christians have to do?", what things come to mind?

❖ Which baptismal promise resonates the most with you and why?

❖ Which baptismal promise is the most difficult for you and why?

❖ Do you ever do difficult things because of your faith? What is that experience like?

❖ How might it change the practice of your faith to focus on the power of God within you?

NOTES _____

_____

_____

_____

_____

_____

_____

_____

_____

NOTES _____

_____

_____

_____

_____

_____

_____

_____

_____

_____

_____

_____

_____

_____

_____

_____

_____

_____

_____

_____

_____

What can **we do,** with God's help?

SESSION 5

How should we read the Bible?

OPENING PRAYER

Blessed Lord, who caused all holy Scriptures to be written for our learning: Grant us so to hear them, read, mark, learn, and inwardly digest them, that we may embrace and ever hold fast the blessed hope of everlasting life, which you have given us in our Savior Jesus Christ; who lives and reigns with you and the Holy Spirit, one God, for ever and ever. **Amen.**

(*The Book of Common Prayer,* p. 236)

Most people believe the Bible is important, but many of us don't read it. Why?

❖ The usual excuses: too busy; it's for other people; we learned it in Sunday school.

❖ We don't know how to read it.

Metaphors for understanding the Bible

❖ Rule book

❖ Operating instructions

❖ Inspirational message

❖ Love story

The Bible is all that and more!

❖ Sixty-six books; a library, collection

❖ Different languages, different writers

❖ Different genres

  – Historical narrative (1 Kings 14:25-31)

  – Law (Exodus 21:28-32)

  – Poetry (Psalm 42:1-7)

  – Prophecy (Isaiah 2:2-4)

  – Narrative (Matthew 4:18-22)

  – Letters/Epistle (Colossians 4:15-18)

  – Apocalyptic (Revelation 6:1-8)

❖ All these differences help us learn to read the
  Bible more faithfully

Because in the midst of the differences, we believe the Bible has a unity

❖ "We call [the Holy Scriptures] the Word of God because God
  inspired their human authors and because God still speaks
  to us through the Bible."
  (The Book of Common Prayer, p. 853)
❖ Not about the authorship but about the inspiration
❖ May not be literal but it's true

How can I read the Bible and discover God speaking to me?

❖ Get the right tools
❖ Set a goal
❖ Start somewhere!
❖ Cultivate the right attitude
❖ Give the Bible a chance

The Bible is not just a book

❖ The Bible is the breath of God (2 Timothy 3:16-17)
❖ The Bible is a living thing (Hebrews 4:12)

Small groups

❖ Have you ever or recently read the Bible? How did it go?

❖ Have you ever read anything in the Bible that has changed the way you act or behave?

❖ Have you ever experienced something that was "true" even if it wasn't factual?

❖ How does it change your understanding of the Bible to think of it as "God breathed" or as a living thing?

NOTES _____

_____

_____

_____

_____

_____

_____

_____

_____

_____

_____

_____

How can I read
the Bible?

SESSION

Does God answer prayer?

OPENING PRAYER

Almighty God, the fountain of all wisdom, you know our necessities before we ask and our ignorance in asking: Have compassion on our weakness, and mercifully give us those things which for our unworthiness we dare not, and for our blindness we cannot ask; through the worthiness of your Son Jesus Christ our Lord, who lives and reigns with you and the Holy Spirit, one God, now and for ever. **Amen.**

(*The Book of Common Prayer*, p. 231)

One of the most frequently asked questions of faith: Does God answer prayer?

Many people understand prayer as

❖ Something we do on Sundays

❖ Something we do by rote

❖ Leaving a voicemail for God

❖ A vending machine

But that's not how the Bible describes prayer

❖ Noah after the flood (Genesis 8:20-21)

❖ Moses and Miriam after deliverance (Exodus 15:1-3)

❖ The psalms record people bringing all their thoughts and emotions to God, good and bad (Psalm 4:1, 5:3, 17:1)

❖ People who encounter Jesus respond in prayer and praise.

  – Mary's *Magnificat* (Luke 1:46-56)

  – Zechariah's *Benedictus* (Luke 1: 67-79)

  – Simeon's *Nunc Dimmitis* (Luke 2:25-32)

❖ Paul urges believers to pray at all times and in all circumstances (1 Thessalonians 5:16-18, Philippians 4:4-7)

❖ James encourages believers to offer prayers, in good times and in bad (James 5:13-16)

❖ And, most importantly, Jesus prays (Mark 1:35, Luke 6:12, Luke 22:41-44)
❖ That's a requirement he passes on to his disciples and to us (Matthew 6:7-13)

Prayer as a conversation that takes place in relationship

❖ It involves both talking and listening as you share your life
❖ It involves times of comfortable silence
❖ It's not always about getting answers to questions or about receiving things

Tips and tricks for making prayer possible

❖ Set a time (when)
❖ Find a place (where)
❖ Keep a list (who/what)
❖ Choose a method (how)
❖ Keep practicing!

NOTES _____

_____

_____

_____

Small groups

❖ What was your childhood experience of prayer? Is that the same or different as your experience of prayer today?

❖ What about prayer is difficult for you?

❖ Does thinking about prayer as a conversation in relationship, rather than questions to be answered, change your understanding of prayer? How so or why not?

❖ Prayer happens in many different forms. Is there a different way of praying that you would like to try? What goals could you set to make that possible?

NOTES _____

_____

_____

_____

_____

_____

_____

_____

_____

_____

Does God meet us in prayer?

SESSION 7

Why do bad things happen?

OPENING PRAYER

O merciful Father, who has taught us in your holy Word that you do not willingly afflict or grieve the children of men: Look with pity upon the sorrows of your servants for whom our prayers are offered. Remember them, O Lord, in mercy, nourish their souls with patience, comfort them with a sense of your goodness, lift up your countenance upon them, and give them peace; through Jesus Christ our Lord. **Amen.**

(*The Book of Common Prayer,* p. 831)

Basically every meaningful conversation about religion addresses the question "Why?"

❖ Why does evil exist?
❖ Why is there so much suffering and pain?
❖ Why do bad things happen to good people?

The question of "Why?" arises when what we believe about God comes into conflict with what we see and experience in the world.

❖ We believe that God is:
  – Omnipotent: all-powerful
  – Omniscient: all-knowing
  – Omnibenevolent: all-loving; all-good
❖ But if God is all-powerful, all-knowing, and all-good, then why do bad things happen to good people? Wouldn't an all-loving, all-good God want to remove all suffering and pain? And if God wants to remove all suffering and pain, wouldn't an all-powerful God be able to do so?

NOTES _____
_____
_____
_____

Why does evil and suffering exist? Christianity has answered this question in a variety of ways.

❖ What goes around comes around; people eventually get what they deserve

❖ People get what they deserve in the afterlife, if not in this life

❖ Evil is merely the absence of good; God doesn't cause evil

❖ Suffering exists to teach us things; evil and suffering have a reason

❖ Evil exists because of human free will

❖ Evil isn't really evil in God's view; humans simply can't see the big picture

❖ God doesn't cause suffering—something or someone else does

NOTES _____

_____

_____

_____

_____

_____

_____

_____

Moving from "Why?" to "Where?"
Where is God when suffering happens?

❖ Bible verses
  – Daniel 3:19-25
  – Psalm 23:4
  – Romans 8:38-39

❖ To the question "Where is God?" Christians proclaim Emmanuel, "God is with us."

❖ As Christians we proclaim that our God became human, lived, suffered, and died an untimely death, so that we would never again have to go through the brokenness, grief, suffering, and death of this world alone.

❖ Where is God when bad things happen?
  – God is with each person who dies, for God has died before.
  – God is with each family who grieves, for God knows the grief and loss of a child.
  – God is with each of us who grieve and question and yearn and long for a world where this is not possible, for God grieves and questions and yearns and longs for that world as well.

First we move from "Why?" to "Where?" And then, perhaps we can ask further questions, those that demand something, not of God, but of us: "What?" and "How?"

❖ What am I being called to do in response to the evil of this world?

❖ How can I respond to the suffering that I encounter?

Small groups

❖ Which of the answers to "Why does evil and suffering exist?" do you find most compelling? Why?

❖ At a time when you were struggling, have you ever had someone give you an "answer" that was unsatisfying or hurtful? What was that experience like?

❖ All of the different "answers" for the presence of suffering and evil are supported by Bible verses. What might the presence of so many different answers in the scriptures say to us? Does it surprise you to see so many different ways of understanding this in the Bible?

NOTES _____

_____

_____

❖ How might what you've heard tonight inform the way that you interact with people who are suffering? What are some ways that we can be with people who are in pain without diminishing or explaining away their experience?

❖ Have you ever had an experience of God's presence with you in a time of suffering or pain (your own or someone else's)? How did that experience inform your understanding of suffering?

NOTES _____

_____

_____

_____

_____

_____

_____

_____

_____

_____

_____

_____

Where is God **when suffering** happens?

SESSION

Where do we go when we die?

OPENING PRAYER

Almighty God, who through your only-begotten Son Jesus Christ overcame death and opened to us the gate of everlasting life: Grant that we, who celebrate with joy the day of the Lord's resurrection, may be raised from the death of sin by your life-giving Spirit; through Jesus Christ our Lord, who lives and reigns with you and the Holy Spirit, one God, now and for ever. **Amen.**

(*The Book of Common Prayer,* p. 222)

We've all seen billboards or heard street preachers talk about heaven (or more likely hell)

❖ Use catchy slogans about heat or smoking and eternity
❖ Emphasize where we're going when we die
❖ Try to instill a sense of fear
❖ Portray belief in God or being a Christian as a means to an end

Most of us wonder about what happens after we die but much of what we have heard comes not from our faith but from popular culture. So what does the Bible actually say about heaven, hell, and eternity?

Hell

❖ Sheol
❖ Hades
❖ Gehenna
❖ Luke 16:19-31

NOTES _____

_____

_____

Heaven

❖ Old Testament: Shamayim—the place where God lives.
❖ New Testament:
  – Echoes the Old Testament understanding; it's the place where God lives
  – It is also where Jesus is from and returns to
  – Jesus, by virtue of coming from heaven, dying, being resurrected, and returning to heaven opens the passageway to heaven (the place where God is) (John 6:35-40)
❖ Actual description
  – Very little
  – Revelation 21:21—streets of gold and pearly gates part of an extended vision or image
  – But neither Revelation nor any other scripture describes heaven as a place focused on comfort and happiness, enjoyment and leisure. Every reference to heaven makes it clear that God is at the center of what's to come.
    • What will be most memorable about heaven is the nearness to God's presence (Revelation 7:9-17)

- Our activity in heaven will not be playing games but joining with angels and archangels and all the company of heaven in the worship and praise of God (Revelation 5:11-14)
- Heaven is not about us as individuals or even the whole of humanity but about the view that through Christ all creation is being redeemed (Romans 8:19-23)

So what can we say about heaven and hell?

❖ Kingdom of heaven
  - Described in parables (e.g. Matthew 13:24-47)
  - Heaven is mysterious, valuable, surprising, and grows rapidly
  - We should pray for it to come
  - It is very near, among us, already here (Matthew 3:2, 4:17, 10:7; Luke 17:20-21)
❖ The rest of the New Testament echoes these ideas
  - 1 Corinthians 2:7-9
  - Ephesians 2:4-7
  - Ephesians 1:9-10
  - Philippians 3:20

"Where do we go when we die?" is not necessarily our best question.

❖ The Catechism poses the question: "What is the Christian hope?"

❖ The response: "The Christian hope is to live with
  confidence in newness and fullness of life, and to await the
  coming of Christ in glory, and the completion of God's
  purpose for the world" (*The Book of Common Prayer*, p. 861).
  – A question about life, as well as death
  – A question about here and now as well as then and there
  – A question about God's purpose rather than our desires
  – A question about the whole world, all of creation, rather than
    just ourselves

❖ The Christian hope is a much bigger hope, a much richer
  promise, than just getting to go someplace nice when we die.

NOTES _____

_____

_____

_____

_____

_____

_____

Small groups

❖ What images of heaven and hell did you grow up with? Where did they come from?

❖ What images of heaven and hell do you now hold? Where did they come from?

❖ What is difficult for you in thinking about heaven and hell? What is comforting to you?

❖ How might it change your outlook to focus on the Christian hope instead of where you will go when you die?

NOTES _____

_____

_____

_____

_____

_____

_____

_____

_____

_____

_____

What is the Christian **hope**?

SESSION 9

Why do I need Church?

OPENING PRAYER

Gracious Father, we pray for thy holy Catholic Church. Fill it with all truth, in all truth with all peace. Where it is corrupt, purify it; where it is in error, direct it; where in any thing it is amiss, reform it. Where it is right, strengthen it, where it is in want, provide for it; where it is divided, reunite it; for the sake of Jesus Christ thy Son our Savior. **Amen.**

(*The Book of Common Prayer,* p. 816)

"Spiritual, but not religious"—a belief that Church is not necessary to the Christian faith.

❖ Belief that church=services
  – Then, if the worship service is flawed or boring, there's no reason to go to church.
❖ Belief that church=building
  – If that's true, then the church is just another building that might sometimes contain or point to God. But there are other equally valid places to meet God, like in nature or on golf courses.
❖ Belief that church is for me, for us.
  – The purpose of church is to make us feel good, so we stop going if it doesn't make us feel good, or if something else makes us feel better.

NOTES _____

_____

_____

_____

_____

_____

_____

The biblical understanding of Church is not about services or a building or something that is "for me."

❖ Holy Temple (Ephesians 2:19-22, 1 Peter 2:4-5, 9-10)
❖ Body of Christ (1 Corinthians 12:12-31, Romans 12:4-8)
❖ Family or Household (Galatians 3:25-29, Galatians 4:4-7)
❖ Light (Revelation 1:10-12, 20; Matthew 5:14-16)

We come to see that Church is not for me at all.

❖ It's for God
❖ It's for others

Church often misses the mark.

❖ Just as marriage is the beginning of a struggle to make love work, Church is a beginning
❖ Not perfect, just forgiven
❖ Communion of sins, forgiveness of saints

NOTES _____

_____

_____

_____

We might move from asking, "Why do I need Church?" to "What is my role in the Church?"

❖ Which stone am I of God's Holy Temple?
❖ What part am I called to be in the Body? What indispensible function do I offer to the whole?
❖ Who are the members of my family, related whether I like it or not?
❖ How can I join my light to the lights of others, that we might testify to the Light of the World?

Small groups

❖ How does it change your understanding of Church to see it as for God or others, rather than for yourself?
❖ Which biblical understanding of the Church is most helpful for you, and why? Which is most difficult, and why?
❖ In what ways does our church fulfill the vision for Church that you heard tonight?
❖ In what ways does our church need to change in order to become the Church that God wants us to be?
❖ How would you answer the question, "What is my role in the Church?"

What is **my role** in the Church?

SESSION 10

Where do we go from here?

OPENING PRAYER

Almighty Father, whose blessed Son before his passion prayed for his disciples that they might be one, as you and he are one: Grant that your Church, being bound together in love and obedience to you, may be united in one body by the one Spirit, that the world may believe in him whom you have sent, your Son Jesus Christ our Lord; who lives and reigns with you, in the unity of the Holy Spirit, one God, now and for ever. **Amen.**

(*The Book of Common Prayer*, p. 255)

Where have we come from? Over the past ten sessions, our questions have transformed.

❖ Can we question our faith? ▶ How can we question faithfully?
❖ Who is Jesus? ▶ Who do you say that I am?
❖ Why did Jesus have to die? ▶ Why did Jesus choose to die?
❖ What do we have to do? ▶ What can we do, with God's help?
❖ How should I read the Bible? ▶ How can I read the Bible?
❖ Does God answer prayer? ▶ Does God meet us in prayer?
❖ Why do bad things happen? ▶ Where is God when suffering happens?
❖ Where do we go when we die? ▶ What is the Christian hope?
❖ Why do I need Church? ▶ What is my role in the Church?

What are we?

❖ We are questioners, God-wrestlers, identities not mutually exclusive with faithfulness.
❖ We are Christians, those who bear the name of Jesus Christ, believing him to be who he says he is—both man and God.
❖ We are saved, whatever metaphor we use to understand that salvation, by Jesus Christ who chose to die, for love of us.

- ❖ We are people called to live in the light of Christ's self-sacrificial love, empowered by the Holy Spirit to embody the reality of our baptismal promises in this world.
- ❖ We are people of the Book, the Bible, understanding that the messy and difficult stories included in its pages are also the Word of God.
- ❖ We are people of prayer, bringing all of our lives, all of our hopes, hurts, love, and anger to God in holy conversation.
- ❖ We are a light in the darkness, a living proclamation of God's love in the midst of the sin and brokenness of the world.
- ❖ We are people of eternity, who live not in fear of hell but in the grip of a Christian hope, which proclaims that we will all be judged by the God of mercy.
- ❖ We are the Church, the Holy Temple, the Body of Christ, the Family of God, the Light of the World, flawed and broken but forgiven and holy, God's people just the same.

NOTES _____

_____

_____

_____

_____

_____

That's where we've come from. That is who we are. So, where are we going?

❖ We continue our pilgrimage, our journey
- Abraham (Genesis 12:1-9)
- The call of the disciples (Matthew 4:19, 8:22, 9:9, 16:24, 19:21, etc.)

❖ We continue with tools for the journey
- The Bible
  - A good study Bible with notes is a great place to start. *The New Oxford Annotated Bible, HarperCollins Study Bible, and New Interpreter's Study Bible* are all great options. Some people prefer a more contemporary rendering like *The Message*
  - *Introducing the New Testament* by Mark Powell
  - *An Introduction to the Old Testament* by Walter Brueggemann
  - *The Good Book* by Peter Gomes or *The Bible Makes Sense* by Walter Brueggemann
- *The Book of Common Prayer*
  - The Daily Office (p. 36)
  - Daily Devotions for Individuals and Families (p. 136)
  - The Collects (p. 159)

- Prayers and Thanksgivings (p. 810)
- Forward Movement's *Forward Day by Day*, in print,
  podcast, app, or online: www.prayer.forwardmovement.org
  Also includes the Daily Office—a great way to follow the
  ancient tradition of saying the Daily Office in modern form.
- *Prayer: Finding the Heart's True Home* by Richard Foster
– Our tradition and history
  - *The Oxford Dictionary of the Christian Church*
  - *The Story of Christianity (Volumes 1 and 2)*
    by Justo Gonzalez
  - *Christianity: the First Three Thousand Years*
    by Diarmaid MacCulloch
– The stories of the saints
  - Lent Madness (www.lentmadness.org) includes
    biographies, quotes, and kitsch from past saints.
    If it happens to be Lent, you can join in the madness,
    voting for your favorite saint in each match-up until
    someone is granted the golden halo.

NOTES _____

_____

_____

_____

- The practices of our faith
  - *Practicing our Faith* by Dorothy Bass
  - *The Heart of Christianity* by Marcus Borg
  - *Celebration of Discipline* by Richard Foster
- Other sources
  - Wikipedia is a good starting place; don't believe everything you read on Wikipedia but don't discount it out-of-hand either!
  - The Episcopal Church's website has a glossary of terms: www.episcopalchurch.org/library/glossary
  - Oxford University Press "A Very Short Introduction" series
  - The New Church's Teaching Series
❖ We don't go on this pilgrimage alone. We have companions on the journey.
  - The community of faith
  - Jesus walks with us along the way (Luke 24:13-35)

NOTES _____

_____

_____

_____

_____

_____

Small groups

❖ What has been the most significant learning for you from our time together?

❖ What questions are you still wrestling with as you continue on your journey?

❖ Which of the "tools" for the journey are you most excited about using, going forward? Which tools seem most intimidating?

❖ What help do you need from your companions as you continue on this journey?

Resources

Session 1

❖ *The Creed: What Christians Believe and Why it Matters*
   by Luke Timothy Johnson
❖ *The Heart of Christianity* by Marcus J. Borg
❖ *Simply Christian: Why Christianity Makes Sense* by N.T. Wright
❖ *Traveling Mercies: Some Thoughts on Faith* by Anne Lamott

Sessions 2-3

❖ *The Creed: What Christians Believe and Why it Matters*
   by Luke Timothy Johnson
❖ *Jesus: A Pilgrimage* by James Martin
❖ *Jesus: A Very Short Introduction* by Richard Bauckham
❖ *Jesus the Savior: The Meaning of Jesus Christ for
   Christian Faith* by William Placher
❖ *Meeting Jesus Again for the First Time* by Marcus Borg
❖ *Mere Christianity* by C.S. Lewis
❖ *The Secret Message of Jesus: Uncovering the Truth that
   Could Change Everything* by Brian McLaren

Session 4

❖ *Crossing the Jordan: Meditations on Vocation* by Sam Portaro

❖ *Let Your Life Speak: Listening for the Voice of Vocation*
by Parker Palmer

❖ *Listening Hearts: Discerning Call in Community*
edited by Suzanne Farnham

Session 5

❖ *The Bible Challenge: Read the Bible in a Year*
edited by Marek Zabriskie

❖ *The Good Book: Discovering the Bible's Place in Our Lives*
by Peter Gomes

❖ *The Heart of Christianity* by Marcus Borg

❖ *Opening the Bible* by Roger Ferlo

❖ prayer.forwardmovement.org

Session 6

❖ *An Altar in the World* by Barbara Brown Taylor

❖ *The Heart of Christianity* by Marcus Borg

❖ *Practicing our Faith* by Dorothy Bass

❖ *Prayer: Finding the Heart's True Home* by Richard Foster

❖ prayer.forwardmovement.org

- *Praying in Color* by Sybil MacBeth, *Writing to God* by Rachel Hackenberg, and other books in the Active Prayer series

Session 7

- *The Problem of Pain* by C.S. Lewis
- *When Bad Things Happen to Good People* by Harold Kushner
- *Where is God When it Hurts?* by Philip Yancey

Session 8

- *The Great Divorce* by C.S. Lewis
- *Heaven: Our Enduring Fascination with the Afterlife* by Lisa Miller
- *Love Wins* by Rob Bell
- *Surprised by Hope* by N.T. Wright

Session 9

- *Church: Why Bother?* by Philip Yancey
- *Life Together* by Dietrich Bonhoeffer

About the photos

Session 1: Streams of light: the central dome bathed in light at Holy Trinity Church (Aya Triada Kilisesi), Greek Orthodox, in Kadıköy, Istanbul.

Session 2: Detail from mosaic dome: scenes from the Baptistry at the Duomo, Florence, Italy.

Session 3: Resurrection at Chora: fresco over the altar in the chapel at Chora Church (Kariye Kilisesi) in Istanbul.

Session 4: Angel on pulpit: detail from the pulpit at the Episcopal Cathedral of St. John the Divine in New York City.

Session 5: Chanting by candle light: Armenians in prayer and procession at Church of the Holy Sepulchre, Jerusalem.

Session 6: Candles in a Greek Orthodox church: candles bear witness to prayer at Holy Trinity Church (Aya Triada Kilisesi), Greek Orthodox, in Kadıköy, Istanbul.

Session 7: Light and shadows in the crypt: at Santa Miniato al Monte in Florence, Italy.

Session 8: Light shines: sunlight shines down on the Aedicule, the building holding Christ's Tomb at Church of the Holy Sepulchre, Jerusalem.

Session 9: Lamps: An array of lamps between the Aedicule and the Catholicon in the Church of the Holy Sepulchre, Jerusalem.

Session 10: Pilgrim walk: Steps worn down by pilgrims to Canterbury Cathedral, England.

Photographer: Scott Gunn

About Forward Movement

Forward Movement is committed to inspiring disciples and empowering evangelists. While we produce great resources like this book and the *Transforming Questions* course, Forward Movement is not a publishing company. We are a ministry.

Our mission is to support you in your spiritual journey, to make stronger disciples and followers of Jesus Christ. Publishing books, daily reflections, studies for small groups, and online resources is an important way that we live out this ministry. More than a half million people read our daily devotions through *Forward Day by Day*, which is also available in Spanish *(Adelante Día a Día)* and Braille, online, as a podcast, and as an app for your smartphones or tablets. It is mailed to more than fifty countries, and we donate nearly 30,000 copies each quarter to prisons, hospitals, and nursing homes. We actively seek partners across the Church and look for ways to provide resources that inspire and challenge.

A ministry of The Episcopal Church for more than seventy-five years, Forward Movement is a nonprofit organization funded by sales of resources and gifts from generous donors. To learn more about Forward Movement and our resources, please visit us at www.forwardmovement.org or www.AdelanteEnElCamino.org.

We are delighted to be doing this work and invite your prayers and support.